I MANIFEST

I MANIFEST

AN ATHLETE'S JOURNEY TO GROWTH

CATE SHEPHERD

• WRITE WAY •
PUBLISHING COMPANY
RALEIGH, NORTH CAROLINA

I Manifest
Copyright © 2021 by Cate Shepherd

Printed in the United States of America
ISBN 978-1-946425-78-2

Book design by CSinclaire Write-Design
Cover design by Klevur

*To all the strong-willed athletes
who want to earn being the best.*

▶ **Contents**

Acknowledgments

Acknowledgments

To my family, mentors, physical therapists, and doctors—I am beyond grateful for your unconditional support and influential guidance. I am so blessed to have such wonderful people in my life. You have prepared me to do big things.

CHAPTER 1

▶ *Prove Them Wrong*

Let me start by making one thing clear; you are capable of impossible things. You can become talented at whatever fuels your fire. I believe that no dream is too big to reach.

Wherever you might be in your life right now ask yourself: Have I set goals that seem impossible? If you have, now is your opportunity to take action and work toward them. If you have never set goals, then it is never too late to start.

Nothing in life is ever given or guaranteed. **I get that everyone is not wired to do the impossible, but everyone is capable of trying.** Dreams can seem crazy, and people might discourage you from trying to achieve them, but why let that stop you? Why let that be the reason not to try? If you are going after your dreams, please go all in! You owe it to yourself to chase your dreams like a hungry lion. Find your hunger. It's somewhere inside you.

I know most people want to reach their goals, and I also know that most people are capable of doing the work it takes to reach them. I know for a fact that if you set your mind on something that makes you happy, you are one step closer to achieving your goal and developing your passion. If you have a passion and a fierce mind, then you should never settle for anything less than your best. You owe it to yourself, and you deserve what you earn from the work you're willing to put in.

One thing that I think about every day is: *I want to be someone remembered for being relentless in my pursuit of happiness. I want to be known as the girl who overcame the impossible. I want to inspire people every single day.* I can't be that person without setting goals for myself that are on the scale of crazy. Crazy meaning when you reach your goal, you are so proud that you never gave up, and you have absolutely no regrets about the work it took to get there. You need to fail, struggle, and be put down so when you reach the top, everyone who didn't believe in you sees that you thrived under pressure.

No person or challenge should ever scare you away from trying. There will always be haters, naysayers, and critics. The way you respond will show your class and humility. You will learn a greater respect for yourself by staying true to your personal journey.

Now I'm not saying you should be alone, because I do believe you can find the right people, the right friends, and the right support team. However, it is up to you to wake up every day and choose to put in the work knowing that people might not like you for it. With that comes the perspective that some people probably won't believe in what you can do. The way I see it, it is simple. They just can't keep up with you.

You are on this amazing ride, and likely most people will never reach your level. Take it as a compliment the next time someone says something rude or critical. It's probably just because they feel intimidated by you and realize deep down that you have achieved at a greater level than they have. Keep your bar higher and don't come back down to their level. When people doubt you, find your inner strength and grit. Use them to continue to lift yourself up.

When I was in fourth grade, I was a little kid with big dreams. I was known to be a "different breed." I was set apart from my classmates in my belief about my future. I was so excited about my passion that I would do crazy things to achieve it. I was that girl! And very proud of it!

When I say that, I mean I didn't care what people said to dissuade me. I looked at things black and white, and I believed my goals were achievable no matter how impossible the vision seemed. I was known as the "Try Hard."

Looking back on it, I am still that! Make sure whoever

you are, you embrace it even if some people view your big dreams as a waste of time.

One day in fourth grade, our history class had a guest speaker. He was a pilot, and he came to talk to us about our future and potential career paths. He went one by one asking each one of my classmates what they wanted to do when they grew up.

Finally, it was my turn. I stood up with confidence and said, ***"I want to be on the US Soccer National Team."*** He paused for a couple seconds. My 10-year-old self was waiting impatiently for a response. He finally replied, "Pick a different one, that is not realistic."

You could feel the silence in the room when he said that to me. I told myself he was silly, that he didn't know who I am, and I tried not to take the poison from his mouth as a criticism. I chose to believe that he just had no idea *who I am!* I stood up again and indignantly said, "I'm not changing it. I want to play on the National Team." I received a glare and no response.

From that day on I did everything I could to prove him wrong, but it was not because I cared one bit about what he thought I could do in life. I did everything I could because I truly believed that I would be honoring my country one day. I didn't care how long it would take. I chose to be relentless and absolutely loved the sweat, tears, and pain that could possibly give me a shot. Granted maybe 1% of the world has a chance to play for their country, but I believed I could. I wanted it so bad that I didn't care what it would take. I had a vision, and I am telling you right now, I knew it was never, ever going to change.

~ ~ ~

In January 2020 at age 15, I was called in to my first US Soccer U-16 girls' national team camp. I made the National Team. I reached my goal and was so grateful to be the woman of strength I am.

If you are struggling to believe that your goal is possible, I promise you it is. Never spend one moment doubting your dream or your journey. What is meant to be will happen. I didn't let what people thought I couldn't do stop me from being a crazy, relentless, driven athlete who actually believed she had a shot at the National Team.

I might be 1% lucky, but I can tell you I'm 99% obsessed, and my relentless and competitive drive pushed me to reach my dream. I had no desire to pay the man back for what he said to me. I chose to be honored by this opportunity. I felt that being humble was more important than being prideful.

Remember, this journey is yours. It will take you to wonderful places if you trust yourself more than anybody else. I am telling you, your ability to pour everything into your passions from your heart can be difficult. I can say that from experience. There were nine other camps before I made my first one. This made it harder for me to believe that I still had a shot, but I never gave up.

One thing you can control is your ability to find joy in what you do. Remember why you play. That is the reason I never stopped. I knew God blessed me with a wonderful gift, and I just wanted to please him and do everything I could to use the joy I have for the game. That was the fuel I needed to be happy with where I was.

It takes strength of character to go against the odds and still believe you are capable. Your ability to have a strong mind can transform your future. Next time someone gives you trash, remember who you are. Your character will be with you your whole life. Accept that there will be people who don't get you. Use their disbelief as motivation to reach the top of your ladder. Remember this is *your* journey, so don't compare your amazing self to others.

You are a completely different flower growing in a completely different garden. You grow and develop at your own speed. Everyone is on a different journey in life, and everyone has enemies, opponents, and critics. Stay true to your ambitions.

There should be no need to listen to people who don't believe in you. Surround yourself with the right people in life and earn every single opportunity life presents to you. Become your own version of Wonder Woman!

CHAPTER 2

▶ *Controllables*

As an elite athlete you want to be in control of everything. You want to feel comfortable with every challenge. You always want to know if you can win that game, and you want the grass to be perfectly cut so you can make the most precise pass.

I hate to break it to you, but most things in life and on the field are out of your control. Things out of your control are things you should not pour your attention into. The best opportunity for growth is when you step out of your comfort zone, and this, my friend, is something that is in your control. If all this was easy, then you wouldn't be elite.

The definition of control is "the power to influence or direct people's behavior or the course of events."

Sounds desirable, right? If not being in control isn't difficult for you, then you might be special. I can say for myself, this is one of my biggest struggles as an elite athlete. I always want to know if I'm going to be successful. It is very difficult to live with uncertainty every day. You can only hope that the things you want will fall in place. I promise time will tell and you shouldn't waste time worrying about it.

One viewpoint worth considering is a saying from my U-16 national team coach, ***"Nothing given, nothing guaranteed."*** If you believe that you have to earn everything, it changes your view on being in control. This can be difficult to live by. Not only in sports but also in life, everyone wants control. It's normal to want control because it implies that you're staying in your comfort zone, which is easy. You cannot grow while in your comfort zone. Most of the time in life and on the field you are not in control of desired outcomes.

How do you handle yourself? I need to say this right now. ***Give up this thought of controlling everything. Give it up.*** When you are constantly focused on a singular outcome, you lose the big perspective. Remember why you play, or for non-athletes, remember what makes you passionate. If you could control everything, then you would not be challenged. You would be living in your comfort zone, and what fun is that? You are not a special human if you stay seated in the comfort of your house. Find your passion and when you aren't in control, embrace the uncertainty.

The day before I left for my first National Camp, I was

nervous, but I trusted that I was called up because I belonged. I trusted that what made me special would show up on the field. At school that day, I could not stop thinking about camp and the experience ahead of me. Apparently, I am human, and that is okay. I was worried and uncertain, but I was also ready to go be the best player I could be. I was ready to use the excitement I had to play at the highest level with the best players in the country. I had the opportunity to really push myself with my abilities to perform under pressure.

During my three p.m. car ride home from school, I received an email from US Soccer. It said something along the lines of:

> *Congratulations on your call up. To make everyone aware of the purpose of this camp, we want you to know we are picking a roster of 20 from the 28 players called in to January Camp to travel to England for an international tournament in February.*

Please realize the amount of pressure I now put on myself just 12 hours prior to my first flight, flying alone, and my first camp without knowing anyone yet. If you know me well, then you obviously know I wanted to go to England. Hands down! Another opportunity had presented itself, and I was hungry for it. I had not even arrived in Florida yet for camp, and all I could think about was England. This was something out of my control, yet I spent the next seven camp days worrying if I was going to be on that plane to England.

Those were seven crucial days that I wasted moments worrying!

I tried to control my ability to make the roster. It was a single focus. I believed that if I scored a great goal or if I had a bad touch, it would affect my ability to go to England. The harsh reality was it was out of my control.

When you want something so bad, it is difficult to keep your focus on the process and the rocks to be climbed, not the prize. To be in Florida that week was an honor itself. My first camp was amazing. The experiences I gained and friends I made were just unreal. The coaches were fantastic and the environment was something not many get to experience.

However, looking back on it, I cannot say I was mentally prepared. I was focused on the wrong thing, which caused me a lot of frustration. My ability to perform at my best felt lost at the point I started worrying about England. I did try to make the best of those seven days though, and I had a wonderful time competing with the best players in the US. It is a true honor to represent your country.

Two days after traveling home from camp, I received no email—meaning I wouldn't be going to England. This was heartbreaking. I chose to get over it and learn from my first experience with the national team. I knew that another opportunity would present itself if I kept getting after it harder. This just proved to me how important it is to enjoy where you are and just be happy with what you are doing in the moment. From this story, I hope you see why you lose the battle when you try to control things.

Please stop worrying about the things out of your control. You have to be okay with the uncertainty. It's part of life. I encourage you to start getting used to your new comfortable. And always soak up all the happiness, excitement, and enjoyment of what it feels like living in a moment. **Some things are out of your control, and that is all right.**

CHAPTER 3

▶ *Own Your Journey*

Every athlete has a responsibility. Your responsibility is no different than your competitors' responsibility. It is your responsibility to be accountable. If you are accountable, then we are friends. I can say right now, if you are accountable, then you are one step closer to achieving greatness. My dad always tells me, "Your ability to be accountable will earn you more respect than you might see."

It makes me so frustrated when people choose to blame someone or something for what happened to them. Your ability to own your journey and your development will be crucial. It will lead you to a successful future.

I know you might think some things that happen to

you are not fair, and maybe you're right. Regardless, you can choose to be the victim or you can choose to accept your challenge or failure and grow. It is convenient when you feel pulled apart by failure to blame your circumstance on the wind and not look at yourself. You could choose to blame your setbacks on COVID-19 or you could look at what wonderful things you have learned, people you have met, and times you have grown.

If you are struggling to hold yourself accountable, find something that motivates you. Find an area of your life that you want to clean up. Things happen in life. Trust me, you're not the only one going through something gritty, and believe it or not, most of the time the people who seem the most happy, successful, and grateful are the ones who have endured the most because they understand what it means to fall down once and get up twice. When I say endure, I mean you have felt every bit of the pain, but you chose to be resilient.

A close mentor of mine has been through 30 surgeries. Do you think she hasn't felt upset? Well, of course she has, but you would never know what this strong woman has gone through, because she is resilient. She doesn't let what some people describe as a failure hold her back. She has become one of the most resilient people on this planet in my opinion. She took her challenges as opportunities to manifest an incredible future.

Another wonderful person in my life has suffered from

many concussions, even to the point of brain surgery to have a tumor removed. This might seem scary to you, but she remembered that with faith no greater than the size of a mustard seed, she could trust God, and she never complained about why this happened to her. She was full of spirit and became one with Christ. She trusted and never doubted her life.

Both of these strong women owned their journey of recovery and trusted the process. They both dealt with the worst, yet both had the courage to rise stronger than most anyone else could have.

I am honored that I have had the privilege to learn from such strong females. If these stories don't inspire you, then you might be living in a coma. **Seriously, to be tougher than nails, it takes every ounce of failure and defeat to come to a place of joy and contentment.** You must have an every-single-day kind of commitment that you owe to yourself to conquer this life and its sharp knives that stab you in different ways.

This type of commitment is found within yourself. Everyone has a fire in them that can light up when they feel pulled down. Yours might not be lit yet, or maybe you have lucked out and never had to deal with controversy or adversity. Not everyone will have an insane story like these women, yet you have the opportunity to get up in the morning with the fortitude to do your best.

Everyone has the ability to strengthen their perspective on life. If you haven't figured it out yet, life isn't all cupcakes and glitter. It has some moldy bread and some dust too. When you feel life is getting difficult, take a moment and ask yourself if you are doing your best and trying your hardest. Are you giving 100% of what you have to offer? This might be doing your best at teaching yourself how to pass a ball, it might be doing your best at being kind to others, or my favorite one said by a friend, it might be "flexing your rest muscles." It could be as simple as finding time to recover and work on being mentally tenacious.

It's fine to feel tired sometimes and to feel the need to rest. Most people think rest is a vulnerability or laziness. For while I thought that. Now having the insight that rest and recovery are crucial parts of an athlete's guide to success, I look at them as an opportunity to heal.

Whatever you do in life, own your development. Leave every ounce of heart in the place you need it most. You never know what tomorrow might bring. I challenge you to make it a goal of yours to be the best version of yourself every day.

One thing that I often think about is who am I to this person? Think about someone in your life you look up to. Take a moment to think of someone you really admire. Why do you feel the need to impress? For me, I want to inspire people every day. I want people to know who I am, not just by watching my ability on the soccer field. As someone once told me, "You are not your sport," so a part of owning my journey is the reputation and standards that I hold myself to. You are so much more than you think. You have so much more in you to give.

Promise me for the rest of your life that whatever difficult things you might encounter, you will choose to fight to overcome them with dignity, courage, and resilience.

Always trust that God has bigger plans for you. One of my favorite Bible-based lessons is that God is preparing each of us for what he has planned for us. What seems troublesome might be what you need to flourish and bloom. To manifest.

CHAPTER 4

▶ *Your Body, Your Engine*

If you want to create an amazing legacy for yourself and be the greatest athlete you can, you never want to lay off. You never want to give yourself a break. There are very few who are addicted to training, fitness, pushups, hour planks, and killing yourself to get results. If you are in that category, though, then you have the most to work on.

Don't get me wrong. Every player would wish to have that drive and desire. I'm that person. I can 100% guarantee that as an elite athlete, no matter what sport you play and what goals you have for yourself, at some point you have hit a point of exhaustion because of your relentless instinct to be superior and push yourself harder when others aren't.

If you feel this, then you know what a craving for hard work feels like. **Wherever you are on the grit scale means nothing if you destroy your body in the process.** Read that again.

As an athlete your body is your engine. And for that engine to deliver, you need to properly give yourself sustained nutrition, mental training, and rest. In order for you to be the rewarding player on the field, you must do these things.

First, nutrition is so important and correlates to your success on the field. I'm pretty sure that everybody has heard, "You are what you eat." You can choose to believe that or not, but let me tell you, as an athlete, you need to be aware of what you put in your body. Food is fuel. Think about it that way. If you are driven, then this piece can't be that difficult for you.

I'm not saying you can't have a cookie once in a while, but I think it is so important to use food as fuel. Your ability to eat heathy is based on the time you take to educate yourself as an athlete. Doing this is responsible. There are so many benefits for athletes with a clean diet. Having a balance is good, and if you want to elevate your game and feel better, then start eating right. Your body is your engine, and for it to deliver, you must feed your body with fuel. It is vital for top performing athletes.

Next is mental training. Believe it or not, soccer is 100% mental. When you're at the top of your game, it no longer comes down to ability. It comes down to who can be smarter, who can make automatic decisions to break down the defensive line, and who can push past their pain when there are two people left to complete the beep test and you are one of them.

Mentality is one of the most solid traits of an athlete. The ability to have composure in times of difficulties or stress can shape you. Your ability to be fully in tune with your body will set you further along than your teammate. Being tough means falling down five times and getting up six. And your ability to get up the sixth time when you are physically drained is your mental capacity to overcome the storm, to defy the odds.

When you are tuned in to your mind, your body is in the same place. Your body and mind are connected. You can be a phenomenal athlete, but if you are mentally fragile, someone will always come along more ferocious. There comes a point where you peak with your ability to kick a soccer ball, but that can't stop you from becoming smarter, more aware, and mentally tougher. I promise you there is always more you can do. If you are someone who is struggling with mentality or even quieting your mind, I have some suggestions for you.

- The first thing I suggest you do is journal. I'm going to preach this because for me being able to look back at the times when I was facing adversity in my life, it makes me realize how capable I am of overcoming challenges and how unbeatable I am.

- The next area to improve is self-talk. Go outside

for a walk by yourself and record your thoughts. Create a video log. This is very helpful.

- Try to sit still and tune everything out. Make the only thing you feel be your body.

- Find someone to become a mentor to you or someone you really trust and talk to them. Some of the best advice you will ever get is from your mentors.

- Play some great music.

- Whatever you need to do to be in tune with your body, do it.

The last important part of being engaged with your body is rest. This one for me is by far the most difficult thing to do. It can be especially difficult when you know people are always out training, always getting better. It can be difficult to find time to rest, but without rest, you can create injuries and setbacks. After you deal with a few injuries, you will realize that your body isn't a robot. You are human, and the body needs rest to recover from difficult training and intense loads.

Recovery is under preached. To be an elite athlete, you must learn the proper way to recover. If that means active recovery, massage, hydration, compression, or ice baths, then go for it. In order for your body to fully recover, you must treat it right.

All of those active things I listed will help, but you

must learn to rest. Rest helps your body grow and prepare for the next training. If you never rest, then you will find yourself with more and more setbacks. And from experience, I would not want that for anyone. If you can see yourself like me at all, then you might understand the difficulties of resting, but I promise you, when you go-go-go with no breaks, it wears on your body until your body gives up on you.

If you need to rest, that is okay. Rest is not a weakness. In fact, if this is something difficult for you, then train your mind like you train your body for your sport to feel satisfied in rest.

For the people reading this who know me very well, you probably don't think these words are coming from my mouth. Because to me, rest is the hardest thing I had to learn. This is proof that every athlete is capable of turning a weakness into a new strength. As an athlete you need your body. You only get one for your whole life, so your ability to take care of yourself will reduce your chance of injuries. When you treat your body right as an athlete, then you will find yourself outlasting the crowd.

I can't tell you that rest will eliminate injuries, because nothing will prevent you from getting in a tackle or keep you from tearing your ACL, but I can tell you that your body has a better chance of outlasting the demands and stress placed on a high impact, high intensity athlete if you take care of your body, including rest. If you learned one thing from this chapter, I hope you remember your body is your engine. If you want your car to travel the farthest it can, then the fuel and treatment you give it has to be better than anyone else's. You are in complete control of this.

CHAPTER 5

▶ *You're Not Done*

Every person has a point where they think they have nothing left to push, that they might be at a lost opportunity, or that a trial is too hard to endure. I'm telling you right now that there is nothing put in your life that is too demanding for you.

You never know how much there is left in your tank until you feel every bit of pain. Your mind can drive you if you're willing to feel every bit of the journey's ups and downs—while appreciating the life and obstacles assembling your beautiful and resilient self.

What in your brain is telling you that you can't do one more push up? What voice can really hold you back from your passion? When did anyone's negative opinion actually matter? If you go down, you better go down swinging. Always give it your all.

I am 100% sure that the human body created by God, the most powerful force of hope in our world, wants you to do your very best. Is that enough motivation right there for you? You might think this is ridiculous, but think about it. You know what it feels like to stop when you're done, even when you knew that you could go more. That feeling is dreadful. You are causing yourself regrets.

This should be the question most athletes ask themselves: Why do I stop? I am hoping that you don't stop. There is so much more weight you can carry. **Things can feel super heavy to lift, but the undesirable hard work breeds gratifying success in your future.** Read that again. There is a whole other level in you that you have not even tapped into yet. A whole other level of will power you have not even discovered.

How could you ever complain about suffering while wanting to be the best? Think about it. You aren't strong without the super draining experiences that have formed the roaring lion that craves more. Am I right? How could you possibly ask for the good stuff without tasting the bad?

When you feel done, I promise you're not. You are worthy, capable, and deserving of every bit of the taste of greatness. You must know that greatness is born from experiences, from suffering, from enduring every challenge and from believing that no one could handle it like you.

You need to make people respect you, and it's not cocky if that is what starts your fire. When you act with authority versus power, then you demand respect. You can't shy away from alarming things. If you're afraid to jump off a proverbial cliff, take the leap. Why hold yourself back from experiencing something new?

You're a beast even if you can't see it in yourself, and I am proud of you for that. You have made it here, but that is just here. You have so much more to see and a beautiful life ahead of you if you push yourself toward your own manifest of personal greatness.

When I write, I write from passion with the hope to inspire you. I don't need a 4.5 GPA to write this. It's just time spent writing about something compelling to me. Hard work does not always mean you're going to be the best. I'm definitely far from the smartest, but I still decided to write this book. I don't care how talented you are. To me talent means nothing if it was easy for that person to attain it.

Read this next statement twice. "I'm going to fail, I'm going to fail, I'm going to fail, but then I will succeed." I hope you know that no one said success is effortless. In fact, it is so tough to capture. You might be the most determined person and still not reach your version of success, but that better not stop you from trying.

You will fail and then brace yourself. You will feel destroyed and then conquer everyone. You have to do the work and whatever that requires of you to breed your craving for success. David Goggin's once said,

"You can do anything if you are willing to suffer." Is he right or is he right? I mean trust me, when you are driven, whatever might be in your path can get obliterated. And there is not one ounce of me kidding when I say that.

If you ever question if the work you put in now will pay off, just look at all the gold medal Olympians, professional soccer players, NBA all- stars, or just go look at someone who inspires you. If you know an athlete, a successful figure, or even a humble human who has had a pain free journey, please come and tell me. I will be waiting my whole life to hear from you.

The things you need to endure to be the best will manifest an incredible future. If you want to be the best, you have to want it that much more. You can't feel bad for yourself or anyone on your journey. Meaning in a respectful way, go easy on nobody. Going easy puts you farther back. Instead of going easy, go harder than you ever have in your life.

Success might not mean that you're #1 or that you get the trophy. But it does mean you're willing to sacrifice everything to be the best version of yourself, and that will be enough. If that is you, then be proud of yourself.

You don't need to be on the cover of *Sports Illustrated* to have an amazing story. Everyone is in a different season, and I can promise you it will get easier. Make a promise to yourself that next time you fall, you will get back up. And remember, you are on a different path than someone else. Do not ever compare your success to someone else's.

If you work harder than you ever have before and pour your soul into your journey while craving the joy you get while doing the work and you can tell yourself that you can't possibly do anymore, then that, my friend, is enough.

CHAPTER 6

▶ *Setbacks Fuel Fire*

Before I say anything else, let me make one thing clear: setbacks are nothing more than a little obstruction in your life. Think about the game of soccer. Someone can obstruct you and cause you to be stuck with no way around a player. Just like soccer, maybe that little obstruction holding you back is there so you can find a new way out.

You can always recover from a setback and grow from it. Many people are afraid of what their setback might lead to or of the duration of pain. The courage to overcome and endure through the toughest times in your life is driven by the amount of resilience you have within. **You must know that there is no setback that can overcome your ability to conquer it.** No matter how draining your challenge is or how hard it causes you to fall, you must always attain the strength to come back to a better place. You might not be in control of what happened to you, but you are in control of the mindset that fuels your recovery.

I feel grateful for the mistakes that have caused my setbacks. Who am I if I haven't fallen? I learned real growth. Stuff happens and you know what you have to do. *Just keep going.* You can take that and run with it in whichever way you might choose.

When you feel like you are suffering or incapable of progress, you are like the little fish swimming in a vast ocean with bigger fish in it. Does that scare you? Or does that motivate you? **What if rock bottom, where you were swimming as a little fish became the solid foundation on which you rebuilt your life?** I truly believe tough times shape you and help you evolve into a person of character that will blossom when the time is right.

I choose to accept that everything that happened to me was meant to hit me because someone else could not handle it. Read that again. I hope you apply this to your setbacks. Just know you can be more brave than most people, and you have what it takes to survive the worst of it in the most unfavorable times. You can choose to be a boss of your failure, and that might be the effort you need to rise above your struggles.

As a high performing athlete, I've already had my first taste of setbacks. Before January 2020, I had never experienced failure, which isn't real life. Now I have.

Before I write about my setbacks, I want anyone who is reading this book to understand one thing first: I am grateful for my sufferings because I have experienced real growth. I do not blame anyone but myself for the hole I dug myself into.

It is June 2020 as I am writing this book and in the last five months, I have some real challenges. Every time I met a challenge, I would just start again with the mindset of a champion. Let me tell you that champion mindset took some time to develop.

It started with a strained hip at National Camp causing me to be less than my best while competing with the best in the country. Then at UNC camp, I had my first knee injury, a mild sprained MCL. That might have changed where I stand on their list, because I had to sit out the whole camp. Then I hit my rock bottom when I found out I was Iron Deficient Anemic. For me to say I was tired, speaks a lot. I felt weak and incapable of completing a simple sprint without burning fatigue in my legs.

After working hard in physical therapy and with my doctors and recovering from these challenges, I began dealing with hip pain. I got an MRI and X-ray to figure out I have iliac crest apophysitis, a labral tear on my hip joint, and a femoroactabular impingment.

Many people might ask me how I dealt with all of that, and being 100% honest, it took baby steps and lost sleep to gain the perspective I have now. It was tough! With the help of a wonderful person, I was reminded that my storm won't last forever. I had never been through a storm like this, and, quite frankly, I'm still in it. It will never be the end for me. It gives me reminders of the resilience I have.

I truly believe that it will get easier someday, just not today. That was something I learned to accept. I have wonderful people in my life who support me and are helping me get through these difficult times.

I need to give my appreciation to my physical therapists, mentors, and my doctor who have guided me incredibly well. In the hardest moments of these challenges, I knew I had the resilience to overcome, the strength to persevere, and the grit to endure the pain.

I always know that there is someone fighting a harder battle, and that in itself humbles me. I feel so appreciative for this period of growth. If you ever fall down, just know that the climb back up will be so worth it. I promise no bad times last forever. Someone once told me, **"Think of it this way, there's no doubt when you're ready to go, you will know with all your heart!"**

The person who said this has gained a fan. This person became like my big sister through all of this. It is so nice when you find someone in your life who becomes your most influential person. When you feel like you are stuck, it is a blessing to have someone to trust. I could not have gotten through all of this without this special person. I gained a wonderful mentor.

This time made me grow, reflect, and trust that my journey will take me where I am meant to soar. The next time you feel stuck and the next time you find yourself in the middle of a storm, remember your purpose. Remember your values and use your weakness as power in your hand to persevere and move forward.

Your past is behind you, you have grown from it. Now you are ready for bigger battles. And the thing is, in my case, even if I could go back, I wouldn't belong there anymore.

CHAPTER 7

▶ *Resilience, My Best Friend*

When I think about resilient people, I see they are the ones who overcome adversity. No matter how long or hard the path or how many odds are against them, resilient people always inspire others with their story of growth.

No one said that being resilient means hard situations are any less difficult or any less painful. Honestly, resilient people go through the worst of it to be proven steadfast. You don't get that title of resilient without proving yourself worthy.

Adversity can be scary, and it can become your enemy. But resilience can be your best friend through scary times. Nobody is born with resilience. It is earned by the number of times you rise up over and over again after you fall. No matter how much you think you are re-living a day because things aren't seeming to get better, I promise things will get easier. Ground Hog Day won't last forever.

One thing that most people don't see is how like-minded resilient people are. I can always pick out the resilient people. You might wonder what sets them apart. It's their ability to overcome difficult situations or their ability to look for the positive when things fall apart. Perhaps you were made for this hard moment in your life to walk through blazing fire and come forth as gold. Resilient people produce positive outcomes and can inspire the world.

When you are resilient you have this competitive drive and rock-solid mentality that you will overcome whatever is pulling you down.

There is no current in life's ocean too powerful for a resilient person. You must not care how foolish or done-in you look while trying to get out of that wave. **You might just need to hold your breath a little bit longer.** I hope that gets you thinking and lifts you up!

When you are resilient, you are focused. That focus is to conquer whatever tough situation you are in. Sometimes in life it isn't that simple, and your resilience might be put into action in different ways. In order to be resilient, you must deal with your problems head on. You never know if you're one step away from turning a corner, if you're one stretch away from no pain, or if you're one step away from your "breakthrough." Meaning you will never know what tomorrow has in store for you until tomorrow comes. Choose to live through today and endure every bit of what you feel. That is why resilient people keep going. You don't know when your breakthrough will happen, but you trust it will.

If you are someone who constantly goes 100 miles per hour, slow down. Remember, all good things take time. I truly believe that some of the most difficult and terrifying times of your life are when you have the choice to start new and embrace the clear path ahead. A clear path doesn't mean you can see your future, it means a new start.

Your story won't fit someone else's, and you might have to be a little more resilient than your neighbor. Sometimes the change you need to make in your life will open new doors. There is always room for change, growth, and improvement.

Resilient people carry that trait with them in every aspect of their life. That is why they always seem so strong and so courageous. **Being resilient in your darkest moments can redefine where the light shines in your life.**

Sometimes the sacrifices you make as an athlete prove how resilient a person you are. Resilience will cause you to find your inner strength that seems hidden in the troubles of trials.

Choosing to be resilient for one moment doesn't make

you resilient. Just like going for one run won't get you game fit. This is something that takes practice. You don't just wake up like you are a boss of your problems if you have never taken the time to feel and hurt through your struggles. This is something to learn.

I can guarantee that the one who chooses to endure will come out resilient, and I mean endure every day. You don't have to be in a devastating loss or injury to be proven resilient. I believe that the most difficult situations produce the most resilient people, but some things might require some passive resilience.

In life you are as tough as you choose to be. You have an opportunity every day to wake up grateful. As an athlete, resilience can get you through a lot. Don't let fear stop you, let it motivate you. Resilient people aren't always loud. Sometimes the people who deal with their problems best are the ones who quiet their minds and feel everything.

I have been blessed to have many people in my life who have been an example to me. Being strong is different from being resilient. When you are resilient you are not afraid of the battle scars.

When you are resilient, that makes you a warrior. So, the next time you face adversity take your resilience in with you and come out a stronger person.

CHAPTER 8

▶ *Find Your Tribe*

As an elite athlete it is so important to have a support system. When I say support system, I mean you need those few people who absolutely love you for who you are and want what is best for you. There aren't many people in your world that will make your "squad," but the ones who do make the cut will be there for you in your most thrilling successes and the days you hit rocks.

You might not have a big squad, and that is perfectly fine. Cling to good people who support you and are there for you on your journey. This will benefit you so much in life. You can't be successful by yourself. Yes, you are the one who puts in the countless hours of work to train and push yourself, but there are so many people who make things come together for you.

I want to thank my family for the countless hours in the car, money spent, and time they invest in me to help me chase my dreams. My dad is my #1 fan, and I never give him enough credit for that. I am grateful for my nutritionist who helped me become educated on the athlete's plate and how to fuel my body. Lastly, I'm beyond grateful for my doctors, physical therapists, and mentors.

I have my tribe. Meaning I have my small circle surrounding me. If you don't have your circle yet, start to build it. I could not be where I am on my journey without my support team. They are the people I would jump in front of a car for. Take the time to let your circle know how thankful you are for them and give them the love and credit they deserve! They are the people who will see you at your worst. It is an honor when you have wonderful mentors surrounding you.

If you think you are alone on your journey, I can tell you right now you are not. There are so many people looking out for you though you may have no idea. So many people have your back. I give so much respect to my doctors and PTs. They know so much more than I do and having the privilege to gain loads of knowledge from intelligent, hard-working people sets you up for success. You can't do it all. Even if you consider yourself to be a super woman.

It is so important to appreciate who your people are. They are the ones who will do absolutely anything for you. All the countless hours they put in to help you is because they love you. They are the ones who will follow your journey your whole entire life. I'm honored to feel so supported through this time and throughout my blessed life.

Knowledge is power when you have people around you who care about your success and can push you. **Sometimes the greatest people you meet might only be in your life when the time is right. But what they bring to you will always be there for you.**

As an athlete it's easy to get caught up in your journey and in your victories and losses, but I challenge you to make sure that your people know how much you love them. You must have so much respect for them.

Many athletes make many sacrifices to do what they love to do, and, believe it or not, they aren't the only ones making sacrifices. Everyone on your support team is. Never ever take for granted those who mean the most to you.

Somehow you will always cling to good people if you stick to your gut. Find the right teammates who love you for who you are, find the right coach who constructively leads you, and find your mentors who become like a big sister to you. When you find these special people, you will know it. The best feeling is when you know how supported you are, and how happy it makes you feel when you get to spend time with them.

Create and manifest opportunities for yourself, do big things, be a brave soul, but remember the people who helped you arrive there.

People will come and go in your life, but don't risk losing someone who means the world to you because you didn't invest time in them and their unique journey. You are surrounded by selfless people who absolutely love when you are happy.

When you succeed, include them in your victories. People and relationships can be as special as you make them. And you must be so engaged in that person's life. Don't ever go through life thinking you did it all.

Continue to shine in all the ways you do, but give credit to the spectacular people who have been and are your inspiration since day one.

CHAPTER 9

Serve Others

As an athlete you have a significant role. You are the reputation you hold yourself to both on and off the field. You are the teammate you choose to be, you are every bit the good sport you act like after a game, and you are every bit an inspiration to the world if you humble yourself before your peers.

As a high performing athlete, many people will start to look up to you, and you should be honored by that. People will come to you for guidance. Never turn them away. I believe one of the biggest compliments an athlete can receive is someone asking them for guidance. When you do good for others, you serve a bigger purpose, but when you serve others, it must be from your heart because you feel so grateful for the opportunity to guide someone.

One of my very close friends from school is an amazing lacrosse player. She is so hardworking, driven, and just outstanding at her sport. This season she is trying out for soccer, a new sport for her to play in addition to her competitive lacrosse. Over the weekend I received a text from her that said, "I've been meaning to ask you this, would you mind sending me some easy soccer drills I can practice? Soccer really isn't my specialty, but maybe one day we could play together, and you could give me some pointers for tryouts."

I felt honored. Being able to serve others with one of my strengths is such a wonderful thing. Sharing my passion and ability to help someone grow and improve made me so excited.

It takes a lot of guts for people to ask for help. If you are struggling with asking for help, do it. Most athletes take it as a compliment to be able to teach someone something they are passionate about. I was so excited about this opportunity to help my friend for tryouts. Now it is my job to give her all the attention and commitment for her to succeed at tryouts. You must know you are going to have fans as an elite athlete. Don't push people away.

There are so many ways athletes can and should serve others. It could be as simple as giving someone a hand after fouling them. Your ability to be a person of character on and off the field will guide you, and it will be a crucial part of your life for college recruitment and in your career.

You can be an amazing athlete and still spend lots of time humbling yourself before your friends, family, and community. If you want to be the best, you must understand one thing. People care about you, and it is critical that they know you also care about them.

Your ability to take time and serve the world can bring you tons of happiness if you let it. Most athletes have a desirable trait that makes them so special—something the world admires from such a committed person, and when I say trait, I mean a useful characteristic. Serving others goes a long way, and being able to share your intriguing journey and passion with those who applaud you might be the reason someone goes for their dream.

I had a wonderful opportunity earlier in my soccer journey to help kids with disabilities learn how to play soccer. I didn't know what to expect. I was a little worried that I couldn't do a good enough job, that my teaching abilities and patience wouldn't suffice.

When I experienced the first day of this camp, I realized how beautiful and unique these kids are. They might be born different, but the joy and extreme optimism that I saw in them inspired me. They have big dreams too, and they had so much fun at the camp. Their faces had beautiful, delighted, shining smiles with joy and elation greater than I have ever seen. These wonderful kids might be the happiest kids on the planet.

My ability to guide them felt so special. The kids just wanted to share their love for the game with someone like me. You never know the ability you have to serve others if you never experience what serving others means. You can have an amazing impact on people. Your ability to serve others can lead you farther in life than your ability to score goals. People coming together for a purpose, regardless of age, skin color, or physical appearance, is a pretty cool way to lead and maybe you become the light in someone's life.

In life, there is no person more powerful than anyone else. Everyone is equal and capable in my eyes. The day I had the privilege to work with disabled kids made me realize I'm no better than they are. They are just as special as I am, and they just want to be happy like everyone else.

In order to be an inspiration in the world, you can't always be seen in your environment of strength, like the soccer field for me. Sometimes being bolder and inspiring people through service to others can do all the talking.

Sometimes being uncomfortable might bring you to a realization: service breeds community and community breeds love. Be the reason someone will want to come to you for help.

CHAPTER 10

▶ *You Are More Than Your Sport*

I want you to ask yourself right now: Who am I? How do other people see me? Pause for a moment and think about those questions. If you considered part of your identity to be something you do, then you need to ask yourself that question again. Who you are is not what you do. What you do is not who you are.

This is something I struggled with after dealing with my first injury. I could not find anything else I wanted to do other than fitness and soccer. You must realize that you are greater than what you do. You could be someone who inspires the world with your service to others, or you might be someone who overcomes difficulties, or you might be a leader. **You can still cling to your passion while pursuing other activities.** I think that is very important because a lot of times people think they need a single focus on one thing, but what they might not realize is how cut off they are when they do that.

Whoever you are, make a list of your traits. It's easy to tell yourself you are what you do because it's something you are good at. You might be excellent at your career, the top of the top, but that is not your identity. Think about this using my case as an example: Do I want to be remembered as a soccer player or for my passion and greater ability to be an inspiration to the world—someone who inspired people every day?

Don't get me wrong, you should feel blessed to be so exceptional at what you do, but start thinking about what makes you so insane. What makes you stand out in a crowd? What ways do you excel at your passion? What makes people look up to you?

I have learned a lot from this. As an elite level athlete, it is easy to be so focused and committed to your sport that you forget you have a life outside of it, but you need to realize you can't play your sport until the day you die, as much fun as that would be.

You might get injured for instance, and if you only find enjoyment in your sport then that causes problems. You might be able to find ways to stay involved in your sport—watching or coaching someone. That is great, but what do you do with the time you had spent training?

Part of being a well-rounded athlete and person is

having more than one interest. It might be very difficult to find something that makes you happy the way your sport does, and it shouldn't have to. Your effort to broaden and expand your focus and daily routine is healthy for you. It might even help you when the time is right to be singularly focused on that game that is your passion. Maybe it's healthy to draw your focus on something else at times, so that your concentration and dedication are that much more personalized and exciting in the moment you return to your biggest commitment in your sport.

You must explore your talents. When I say that, I mean think about what you could do when you can't play your sport. Being more than your sport is a bigger commitment than just finding more interests that make you a well-rounded person.

You can be an inspiration to the world by the way you act outside your sport. Are you humble? Are you kind? Going back to what I said in the beginning of this chapter, what do people see you as? I am a big believer in hard work, dedication, and personal drive. You can easily connect your commitment and drive from your sport to being the best you can be every day, constantly setting an example and setting standards.

Be the leader on and off the fields. Who I am outside of soccer is greater than my ability to master a shot. I use my heart and passion to inspire people. One goal of mine every day is to thrive with my hard work and grit while humbling myself by my accomplishments to focus on how I'm an inspiration to people.

Someone once emailed me and said, "Everything you put on your story for soccer shows how hard you work and how much you want to reach your goals. Anytime I'm feeling down about lacrosse I go on my Instagram to see your story and it pushes me to workout. You have been such an inspiration for people you might not even know."

Let me make one thing clear: it isn't my soccer ability that inspires people. I hope you know that. Anyone can be good. That means nothing. It is the example I set by my actions and characteristics that inspire people. My dedication by being someone more than a soccer player will carry me way farther in life.

When you realize that your ability to be someone super special has no effect on the crazy monster you are on the field, it will show you that it's healthy to attain both extremes, but each in the right situation. Sometimes understanding that can be difficult, but remember your purpose in life is greater than your ability to be an elite athlete.

Whoever you might be, go be the best you. Whether you are playing in a championship game or speaking at a ceremony, or living daily life, **who you are and what you say must reflect who you want to be.**

CHAPTER 11

▶ *Patience Manifests Opportunity*

One of the most difficult things for athletes to learn to cope with is being patient—especially when you are aware of other people putting in hours and hours of training, absolutely grinding with pure heart. Having to be patient can be so annoying, but let me tell you, maybe because you waited, a new door opens. Or maybe because you chose to let your body recover from an injury, you reach a whole other gear.

One reason why every athlete must learn patience is to display composure and self-control. As athletes, sometimes waiting is very stressful. You might be waiting to hear if you make the roster, or you might be struggling to master a skill. Whatever it is that you are waiting for, it is important to train your mind to be okay with the discomfort waiting brings. Find something that might keep you busy while waiting for your answer. In regard to training, it can be super frustrating when you just can't seem to master that drill. Don't be too hard on yourself. Any good thing takes time and practice.

You need to realize that patience is crucial. If you don't believe in patience, then I can imagine you have impulses. This is something I struggle with. It's hard when an opportunity presents itself not to react immediately, but I'm telling you that the thing that you said no to might give you an even more remarkable experience.

A person in my life I think very highly of said to me, "Patience means not rushing the process, sitting with the discomfort and not acting on discomfort to make things happen faster." When you feel discomfort from someone or something, it can cause you to act quickly. I truly believe patience will allow the right thing to happen at the right time.

Every good thing has a cost, and maybe your cost to receive that super spectacular thing is formed from the time you spent waiting. Read that again. If you learn to embrace your uncertainty and sit with it, you will make progress.

Trust me, patience is one of the most difficult things to get good at. But you must realize that with all good intentions, God might have something better for you. **What if waiting with the discomfort of not knowing manifests a future of joy, success, and prosperity?**

You might need to view your patience as a belief that things may happen in a different way than you thought and learn to adapt to the change. **The wait you are in, or the quiet season where you feel no good is being produced, might be the time where everything is aligning for your future.** Read that again. Your ability to overcome your uncertainty will cause you to be patient.

Every great thing that has happened in your life took time to develop. You didn't wake up smart or wake up good at soccer. You worked hard, and that determination created opportunities. Just remember those opportunities didn't present themselves until the timing was right. Find joy in being completely present.

CHAPTER 12

▶ *Embrace Your Spark*

Every athlete has one specialty. Something that causes them to be exceptional. Something individual and unique to them that causes them to shine. When you identify yours, this is "your" trait. It might be your impressive technical ability, maybe it's your ability to take leadership, or perhaps your ability to tune out everything. Whatever this special trait is, you must embrace it. This is your magic, and it is something that you can be very proud of. It is something that has brought you much success. This specialty of yours is also known as your "signature."

When you have something that no one else has, that itself makes you powerful. It might draw you attention or be an inspiration to people.

Everyone has one thing about them that people would strive for! Even if you believe that you don't have a "secret" potion or magical wand that makes your special ability shine and come to action, you do. You might need someone to help you find it or maybe it's in the process of becoming phenomenal.

There is something to be said about insane athletes. To fill a roster of 18 players, the coach looks for that spark or special talent a player might have. Your greatest ability could be used to your advantage when filling a specific position.

When you have this special trait, it can guide you to wonderful leaps in your journey. You have some magic in you that is so good, and it is something that makes you proud. It is something no one else can do as well as you.

Maybe you worked hard for this special magic or maybe it's natural to you. In order to be the best player you want to be, you must embrace that one thing that lights a fire on the field. If you can't find your "specialty," then search your talents. Think of something you do that people might admire or something that brings you so much joy because you know you are a boss at it. That one trait that you see college coaches writing down in their notebook.

My specialties are my work ethic and my dynamic dribbling. Since work ethic is one of my best strengths in soccer, this is where I need to use it to my advantage. It is something people might not fully understand.

How can someone be so good at pushing through physical fatigue and using this motor that never runs out of fuel. This is something I have to my advantage. I'm willing to work 100 times harder than anyone else if it means I get more out of it.

For example, at my academy practice we will perform a drill that is a competition. There is a winning team and a losing team. If you are on the losing team that means you are getting on the line, but for me, regardless if my team wins or loses, I'm on that line for sprints.

Something you might not know about me is I'm obsessed with fitness. You might think I'm crazy for wanting to run a beep test every day, but this is why I never run out of gas on the field. This is why my work ethic and relentlessness is so incredibly high, because I'm never fully satisfied.

As you can see, your ability to use your strength as power will become a wonderful influence to others. Now it might take time and people might not get the inhumanness of your "specialty," but if that is how you make yourself better, then use it to your advantage. People might not realize how your specialty pushes them to be better than if you weren't there. I can tell you right now, some special traits in athletes can make people fear them or feel inferior to them. If you are great at something, you deserve to let your talent shine but in a humble way.

I can tell you it took some time for my teammates to know that I don't do the extra fitness to be a "try-hard" or "cocky." This has been something difficult for me to overcome. I know for me that this thing that makes me so good is from pure joy. I do it for no other reason than pure happiness. Usually something you are incredible at is most likely something you love doing.

I find joy in extreme fitness, and I wouldn't want it to be any other way. Because of that, some people might think I just want to show off. I can tell you right now the work I do is for no other benefit than for myself. I find enjoyment from pushing myself to be better. Some people just don't get it.

My coach has a running joke with my team for when we do fitness. He says, "We will have 3 lines. Line 1, Line 2, and Cate's line. Meaning there was Cate's line because no one wanted to run against me. Now the reason I'm sharing this is because if that thing that sets you apart from the crowd causes people to fear you, that might not be a bad thing. **People will respect you when they realize the talent you have is born from your relentless hours of training when you decided to do more than everyone else.**

Some people might never get it. They might always think that this special ability is just pride speaking, but what most people don't understand is that those who light that spark in themselves are living to their capability. Your joy in doing what makes you the best should inspire others. Find what makes you insane and use your magic to breed your future success.

CHAPTER 13

▶ *Handling Pressure*

When I hear the word pressure, the first thing I say to myself is that pressure is a privilege. When you are in a high-stress, high-impact environment, you *forget to remember* that the pressure is only from people with high expectations because they know you are a talent. It is very overwhelming to see pressure for what it is as an athlete and face it head on. It is very important to remember how pressure is a compliment in a way.

You might not see it that way, but if you have a lot of spectators or have an expectation to perform at a certain level that means you are valued. No successful athlete who deals with pressure hasn't been intimidated by it at some point in their life. A lot of times athletes might be recovering from injury or experiencing a downfall in their season. That in itself brings a lot of pressure on the athlete to get where people think they should be or at a different speed than they want. If you learn to accept the pressure of being an elite athlete and your ability to overcome and prove to the world that you belong, then pressure will no longer be a scary thing.

Many athletes don't make it to the top because when they experienced pressure, they felt the need to remain in their comfort zone. I can tell you pressure produces growth. It can be hard to see if you are failing to accept it, but the rewards of dealing with the terrifying pressure in the moment will grant you more growth and success than choosing to settle for what feels comfortable.

Morgan Harper Nichols once said, "Amidst all the pressure to keep going and to keep going, may you also take the time to learn the art of being; being loved, being held, being seen, being in the presence of the one who calls you to rest. For beyond your accomplishments, and your calendars, and your lists, you were made with purpose and intention to reflect the glorious light to abide in love that reminds you even in the pause you are still where you need to be." Pressure should never cause you to lose control of your beautiful life. You might not be ready to deal with the pressure and demands of being an elite athlete, and that is okay.

Growth takes time, and gaining control and composure through pressure takes experience. The ability to rest with ease and embracing pressure will set you up for success. You might not be ready for this, but time will tell. Not all athletes are in control. When they lose composure or feel they can't control a situation, or someone gets in their head, they will fail to use that pressure to their advantage.

From my experience, the most important piece of advice I can give you on how to deal with pressure is preparation. Preparation is key. Whatever you need to do to get in your zone, to prepare yourself for the demands of any game, you must learn how to prepare properly. If you know that you are playing striker against the best defender in the country with US scouts and college coaches coming to your game, you owe it to yourself to be prepared for that pressure.

If you are going to succeed in high pressure environments and excel, you must prepare your mind for complete control of your thoughts and actions on the field. You must be fully aware of the situation. You are not in control of the score of that game or the quality of grass you are playing on, but you have every bit of control over your mindset and mentality going into that game.

Everyone has a different way of preparing, and that is totally acceptable. Whatever works best for you must become a habit, so when things do not go as planned, you can adapt to an environment of high stress and pressure to perform. When you are in a situation to perform and showcase your abilities, you must remember the joy you have when you play. Don't let dynamics out of your control interfere with your ability to play for the fun and love you have for the sport.

Next time you are under pressure, use it to your advantage and remember you are valued. Pressure brings a lot of attention with it, and that can be misleading sometimes. Do not get caught up in the attention of the elite level where you play. Remember that you owe it to yourself to always play the beautiful game of soccer for one reason—the desirable joy produced from your heart.

CHAPTER 14

▶ *Strides Means Stamina*

Let me start by saying, your ability to improve is greater than your ability to achieve perfection. No single person on this planet is perfect, yet so many people base their progress off perfection. If you become "perfect" at something, then your goal was set too low, and it was too easy for you. The thing is, you are not perfect, nobody is.

Achieving perfection in anything is impossible. You might disagree with me, but even if you became so incredible at something, like you are a boss at your level, you are insane, an absolute achiever, and total freak, I still think that's not perfection. You could do so much more to improve whatever your talent is. There is always more you can give. I don't believe in perfect people. The word perfect isn't in my dictionary.

If you are "perfect" then you consider yourself done. Are you ever really done? Read that again and think about it.

Now the reason I started with that is because I want everyone one to know that being perfect isn't what you want. What you want is progress. And progress is way greater than perfection. When you become "perfect," then you can't make any progress. Start aiming for strides instead of perfection. When you make strides you make progress, and progress means you keep growing. Embrace the fact that you are making strides. Strides means growth and growth means success.

The definition of being perfect is "a person or thing perceived as the embodiment of perfection." I believe that no one can truly reach their capability until they learn from mistakes, missed opportunities, and times they tripped over a rock. It's okay to be human. If you trip over a rock that doesn't make you imperfect. It just means you were given another chance to find a new way around that rock.

If you want to be a successful athlete or person, **start loving your imperfection.** That imperfection is where growth occurs and when you make strides and improvement, it's where you gain stamina to sustain prolonged physical and mental effort.

Effort to become the best you can be doesn't mean that you will become perfect. Your ability to make strides from where you were last season is success. If you couldn't run five miles in July but in August you ran six, then that right there is progress.

You might be recovering from an injury and yesterday you could do no weight bearing on your right leg, and then today you did two single leg RDLs. That is progress. You should always aim for progress with the mindset that you can always get better, always push yourself harder, and always think smarter. If you believe you can't physically run more, then start training your mind to overcome. There are always ways to improve and grow.

Trust me, if you were perfect, you would have no reason to get up in the morning and train harder, reach higher. Be grateful for your imperfection and believe that you will make strides. Success is a choice and those who make it the farthest on the journey always believe there is more they can do and more they have to give.

Your ability to crave improvement is more impactful than your ability to wish for perfection. Think about that. Trust the work you put in and aim for constant strides. Make it your goal to never peak. Always know your abilities at heart and use your talents to breed constant growth.

> ## *Smart > Hard*

Being able to push through impossible things makes you hard. Being hard can be a compliment. When you are known to push through pain, you like being known as "unbreakable" or "indestructible."

There comes a point where going hard might lead you to a setback or injury. **There comes a point where being known as the "impossible" or "the person who feels nothing" can create negative outcomes and expectations in your life.**

Having good balance is very relevant to creating a successful future and being able to maintain healthy stamina, but in order to achieve that greatness, you must be smart. Yes, the ability to overcome pain is super valued, but when you take it to an extreme, then it will cause you setbacks. There is a balance to everything, and when it comes to training and not overtraining, you need a good balance between rest and when it's time to go hard.

If you live in your own world thinking that you can only be in "go hard time," then you aren't being smart. This is something not many people struggle with. Most people value their rest time. I guess you can consider me a rare species that hates rest.

I just want to physically push myself so much every second of every day. I always try to make things harder for myself, even if it means taking the stairs instead of the elevator at the airport. My ability to push through pain has caused me setbacks that forced me to rest.

What I have learned is that rest is the medicine your body needs to recover. It is so important to find a good balance in your life between hard and smart. Being hard and smart are both wonderful traits if you use them correctly.

I used to believe that smart meant pushing hard till you can't, but I was wrong. Smart is when you make the decision to be tuned into your body and listen when you need rest. I will never forget how long it took me to grasp this, but someone very special taught me, "This is your body, your journey."

Think about this. Whatever path you might be on causes you to be in tune with yourself and your ambitions. You must be accountable for your mistakes and learn from them. **Being smarter is greater than being hard.** Anyone can be hard. Being hard is like a shield, and anyone can wear a shield and act tough. But few can use intelligence to say "no" once in a while.

Being smart about your body and the rest you might need will then propel you to go hard at full force, but smart should always come first. You can hurt your future if you don't listen to the voice telling you that you are done, and in some cases, it's okay to be done. Everyone is taught the perspective, "Push until you pass out," and that is not always what might be smart. Smart means feeling every bit of pain, being able to acknowledge it, and telling yourself to stop. Stopping doesn't always mean giving up. Read that again so you will remember it.

Being honest, I used to believe the "push until you pass out" perspective. I thought that if I didn't push 100x past my tiredness, then I was weak and soft, but let me tell you I'm far from that. **My ability to tell myself to rest takes a lot more strength than the extra sprint I do for fun.**

It's smart to give yourself a break. You need to preserve your body. When it is never fully recovered, you can never give your best efforts. Next time you feel tired, "flex your rest muscle" as my friend said. Consider that being smart means giving your body the time it needs, and then you can go all in with all your heart.

> ## *Why Are You Still Going?*

When your sibling hits you in the face with a pillow causing you to fall off your couch that makes you furious. I'm pretty sure that it is safe to say you get right up and hit her in the face even harder, but that might just be a sibling thing or me talking.

Regardless of where you are in your life and what adversity sneaks up, you have the choice to keep going. If you have the ability to get hit in the face by your sibling and get back up, then you can do the same thing with life. Rise above it.

Walk through the fiery flames and come forth as ice. Meaning, you won't melt through all the adversity. No matter how hot the flame is, you must not let it bring you into the heat of failure. Failure can be a burden but don't let that be the reason to stop. **You have the capacity to endure the heat, feel it, yet not be melted by it.**

Every day you have an opportunity to wake up with the courage to face whatever demons might strike. That might be the reason you keep going. You might be inspired by someone, you might be fighting back from an injury, or you might have massive dreams for yourself. **There are countless reasons why you should keep going, and a lot fewer reasons to give up.**

You must want it for yourself. That should be the fuel to keep going. When you are doing extra training and others are sleeping, that is dedication. When you put in 50 more draining minutes than your teammate, it means you kept going when others stopped. You craved the success, and you know that your success requires your ability to keep going in the toughest moments of life.

I believe one of the most difficult times in your life is when you ask yourself, "Why am I still going?" I can reassure you that your comeback is stronger than your setback. When you feel exhausted, you must find that gear to push through, you must never give up the fight. The reason you are still fighting might be the reason something incredible presents itself. It is very difficult in the busyness of your life to know that your outcome will be glorious if you get through difficult times.

Three years ago in December, I was attacked by a German Shepherd while sleeping over at a friend's house. It happened at two thirty in the morning. It was pitch black dark. I was fighting, punching, protecting myself. I was screaming while feeling the excruciating bites from the dog piercing my skin. After about two minutes, I was still fighting. I didn't know why there was no help yet, but I kept fighting. I told myself, "Cate, it's you against the dog." With a few more draining punches, I was out of it.

The next minute I see the lights on and the dog no longer on me. I was lying on the floor against the couch in the worst pain I have ever experienced. I had blood pouring out of me. With about 16 different puncture wounds, bites, and teeth marks, I was so weak I couldn't even stand up. As my friend's parents lifted me on to the couch, I went into shock with every part of my body shaking uncontrollably.

My parents got to my friend's house and my dad came in. He wanted to carry me to the car to drive me to the ER. Stubbornly I said, "I want to walk." With the 16 teeny Band-Aids on my wounds, I got up to walk to the car. Immediately blood started gushing through the Band-Aids. That meant I was no longer allowed to walk. We made it to the ER, and by five a.m., I was home resting in my bed.

Now, I could have given up in that fight, but I knew I had more left in me. Granted, I might have been hallucinating by the end, but if it meant I would come out alive, then I wasn't going down without giving my best fight. I don't think the question "Why are you still going" entered my head once because I knew I wasn't going to give up.

Next time you feel every ounce of you is drained, you must find your way out. I promise there are always reasons to keep going. Whatever drives you to carry on in life will guide you to keep going. And when another battle appears, you keep going again. The reason to keep going may be difficult to accept, but the humbling growth should certainly be the reason you move on in life.

You are in a constant game with your mind. It can be super difficult to tell yourself to keep going. Your mind has the ability to overcome crazy things if you fight the urge when it tells you to back down. You will have your fair share of adversity in life. That is real life. Please always remember you still keep going because you have a wonderful purpose and a bright future ahead of you. Be proud of yourself for getting up again and choosing to carry on with your life.

CHAPTER 17

▶ *Faith the Size of a Mustard Seed*

Having faith only the size of a mustard seed could bloom your life in the most beautiful way. God created every human in his likeness and image. He loves us as his children, yet he still will let us enter into our darkest places. You might be someone who struggles to understand why God would allow you to go to a place of fear.

God lets you go into the storm weak, yet most people come out strong. That is because you were never alone. When you start to believe you are alone, at war with yourself, then fear can overcome any proper decisions to remain steadfast.

One of the most difficult things is understanding why you went through that storm. Some people choose to find out for themselves, but you can rely on God through prayer to find answers. Even when you feel like there is no answer or you feel ignored, you are not being ignored and perhaps you don't see the answer given. You might be thrown into a new problem by yourself because you need to get your feet wet first, but that doesn't mean that God isn't right next to you through it all.

Your faith can guide you through your whole life. It will be the light in the dark, and the height you need when you are at your low. Trust that as with everything, you must wait. Maybe your season isn't done yet. Accept that. **You have to believe that the most difficult times in life are just the preparation for what God has already prepared for you.** Read that again and ponder it. Your suffering will help you become complete and mature, lacking nothing.

As an athlete, your faith can bloom at any moment. You don't have to go to church every week to become one with Christ. **Your ability to use your faith to overcome fear and pressure can take some of the pain away from difficult situations.** Know that you might just need a little faith to then find the joy and comfort in the discomfort of life.

I can tell you I believe God is the only one who knows your future. He holds your future in his hands. That should make you feel worthy of the Lord. The chapters in your book are already written. Granted you might be on chapter 7 and maybe it is the rising action in your life, but maybe soon you will reach your life's climax and good things will come to you.

As difficult as it can be to see, remember that God loves us enough to descend with us into dark places and produce in us a true steadfastness as we come back into the light. How powerful is that? You must know your suffering does not last forever. Your ability to overcome it does.

In the most defying time of my life, battling through all my setbacks, I took my faith to another level. I spent time with scripture and prayer trying to understand why I'm here. Let me tell you, without my faith my whole perspective was screwed up. My new understanding to use my faith as power to overcome adversity has been something humbling to me.

I never knew the power of prayer until I spent many hours doing it. Some of the answers I needed were revealed to me when I needed them most. I finally felt at ease in my suffering, knowing that I was being protected by God, and I found joy through the worst of the hard times.

God's love for us is unconditional. He forgives willingly and loves unconditionally. I promise you there is no greater force of love and comfort than what God will bless on your heart.

If you are really struggling right now or dealing with suffering, I highly encourage you to find some time alone and read the book of James in the New Testament. This is my favorite book in the Bible. In James 1:2-4 it says, ***"Consider it great joy, my brothers and sisters, whenever you experience various*** *trials: because you know that the testing of your faith produces endurance, and let endurance have its full effect, so that you may be mature and complete: lacking nothing."*

One thing I have started doing when I go through a trial is to write the date it happened above this quote in my Bible. When I read James now, I see the marks of my setbacks as times I reminded myself to endure.

You deserve what it feels like to be protected. Choose God to be your source of protection, and your choice will guide you on the field, in life, and on your journey.

CHAPTER 18

▶ *Consider Yourself a GOAT*

Let me start by making one thing clear: you are so amazing, but that is something I'm telling you. **In order to be a literal prodigy of pure greatness you must believe that you are amazing.** You must be confident enough to consider yourself a GOAT. For those of you who don't know that term, it means Greatest of All Time. Start considering yourself a GOAT. You might be the GOAT at soccer, or you could be the GOAT physical therapist. It doesn't matter what you are the greatest at, but own it. It shouldn't matter what people tell you. It's up to you to believe it.

This might sound funny, but my mom is the GOAT at making toast. When she toasts the bread, it is perfect, yet I continue to burn mine every time. She still makes me toast to this day. My point is, you might be the

GOAT of seemingly pointless things, but to be farther ahead than your opponents you must believe that you are the greatest at something.

Start complimenting yourself more than tearing yourself down. Your ability to breed positive thoughts starts with your ability to know you are great. You must be happy with yourself. **Start trying to better the person you are rather than wasting time and energy on wishing you were someone else.** Be able to look in the mirror and tell yourself that you are on fire right now. Be able to look in the mirror and be pleased with who you are becoming.

In soccer or any sports, to be the best you have to think you are the best. You almost need to hype yourself up sometimes. You are worthy of achieving awesome things, but it starts with the belief that you are capable of it. Too many times athletes see other athletes doing amazing things, and they doubt their ability to do the same. No matter who you are or who you are up against, you must tell yourself that you are better than that person.

When you start acting like a boss, people respect you. People view confident people as leaders, so when you own your talent and believe that you are great, then you will naturally feel stronger than other people. The way you walk on the field and the way you walk off the field can contribute to this.

Let me make this clear: there is a big difference between believing you are great and being cocky. **When you get**

to the point of being cocky, whatever ability you had to be great goes away. Being cocky isn't what I mean when I say you are great. In fact, the most talented and GOAT athletes have received that badge because of their humility to earn everything.

Everyone has an opportunity to be bold and confident, and everyone has the ability to let that do the talking. You don't need to tell people how great you are. The belief I am talking about is something that should be kept inside you.

When you believe you are the greatest, that can help you have the confidence to meet your expectations. Don't get me wrong, you can't be the GOAT of everything. This is something that develops over time and this feeling of being the GOAT is something that needs to be kept inside your heart. It is perfectly healthy to believe you are the best to fuel your progress, but always be humble.

I believe you can be confident and humble at the same time. Being humble means you don't boast in your accomplishments. Start being a GOAT while showing humility. Your actions speak way louder than words. You don't need your mouth to make your greatness known. It's what you do to humbly receive the accomplishment as an honor and move on to the next challenge.

CHAPTER 19

▶ *You vs. You*

Stop competing with people who are on different paths. The only person you should ever compete against is yourself. Make each day better by trying to grow and learn from your mistakes that happened yesterday. When you start comparing yourself to others, you get off track, and when you get off track, you get caught wishing instead of living. It is important to be focused on being the best you every day.

You won't get anywhere quicker by trying to do something someone else can do. You need to accept the fact that you are on a completely different road. Sometimes your drive might be a little slower with some detours. Maybe someone else just rides the highway. Your journey is designed to be different. You aren't meant to be the same as someone else. **When you start basing your**

progress off someone else's success, that will cause you to fail.

At my first team meeting with the National Team we were told: "You are climbing your own ladder to reach your own potential, and that will look different than your teammate sitting next to you."

Think of today as a better version of yesterday. When you are persistent in the work you do to develop, it will pay off. When you compete, you must compete to be your best, with all you have to give, and be the best version of yourself.

You have made many sacrifices to get to the place you are now. That is from your development. You need to start personalizing your journey. Admire the hard work you did to help you arrive where you are. Five traits that will help you attain your goals are *responsibility, initiative, humility, self-belief,* and *growth mindset.* When you stop worrying about the people ahead of you and start making your own type of progress, then you will see those traits in yourself.

Your ladder of potential is guided by the work you put in to strengthen your abilities. To get to the top of your ladder you must tune out all of the fatal distractions. **Let the work people do be motivation to you, but don't let it become your reality of what you need to do.** You could be head on with someone competing for a spot your whole life, but then suddenly your path starts to change directions, and that, my friend, might be what you need to see to find yourself again. Maybe the reason you go on your own path is to bring you more joy than you could have imagined.

Start focusing on your own growth. Indeed, things might not make sense or might seem unfair, but I'm telling you, it is your opportunity to make the next path and next opportunity the best, and that could be your hope for greater happiness and growth. Trust the process.

One day I came across this story though I can't remember where. It was a dialogue between two flowers. The sunflower said, "I love your petals." The daisy replied, "Thanks! I feel like I'm blooming way slower than you though." The sunflower replied, "We're different flowers, silly!"

Remember, you are special and growing at a different speed than your competition. How can someone so different be your competition? The need to compete can turn into a contest. When things turn into a contest, you can lose the enjoyment. Instead of competing with someone, work on yourself. Compete and go hard on yourself, but don't waste time getting caught up with something or someone you haven't become yet.

CHAPTER 20

▶ *Pure Heart*

The best piece of advice I can give you is follow your heart. If you are passionate about something, I encourage you to chase your dream. No matter how talented you are, or the level of athlete you are, it shouldn't matter. **The only thing you should crave is your aspiration for unexplainable joy doing what you love.** Everything else, good, bad, and in-between, will maneuver its way in. If you spend the majority of your life living with hope and you dream big, then give yourself a hug.

As you take leaps and bounds in your development, things can start to get too serious. Don't let big things scare you, and certainly don't forget why you play. When you start to feel overwhelmed with the many expectations people have for you, it's easy to forget the joy the little five-year-old you felt when you were kicking a ball around back where it all began. Or the joy you felt when you would laugh at yourself for tripping over the ball. You should never have to lose that joy no matter how much pressure is bestowed on you.

As you start doing big things in your life, go into everything you do with heart. If what makes you passionate means putting in extra work to accomplish it, then I want you to find the most joy possible doing it. Your ability to pour your heart and soul into your passions will create the stamina to manifest your future. You will find more success when you spend time doing something you love.

Follow your heart. The cool thing is your heart knows where you want to go, and it will lead you to your destination. Let your heart guide your actions, and wherever you travel to do big things, let your heart, the strongest muscle in your body, lead the way. Your ambitions and aspirations are formed from your heart.

Everyone has this crazy ability to love something so much that it becomes their passion, and whatever that might be for you, I hope you use your soul to find the times of your life where you have pure happiness. Being happy is what is most important. **If you are happy with what you are able to do, that, my friend, is considered a blessing.**

CHAPTER 21

▶ *No Final Destination*

If you think you've landed, you probably have another flight to catch. Think about it. You could end up in a place you think is the end. I'm telling you it's not. Life changes, and one thing I can tell you is trees keep growing. There is no final destination in life. In fact, most of the time when you feel satisfied, another opportunity presents itself.

If you are an athlete who just went pro to play soccer as a job, that is indeed a destination, but that is not the final one. When you think there is no other opportunity, I can guarantee there is. You will never reach your final destination until you go to heaven. Life is full of possibilities, so if you didn't get the outcome you wanted, then most likely a new one will present itself.

If you believe that there is no such thing as impossible, then your destination will always change, because you will always have a better place to go.

I encourage you to never settle for anything less than your best. Your life is full of curve balls, and maybe the one that you don't see coming hits you in the face. Let it hit you. Next time you will see it coming. You learn from not seeing clearly and being surprised that you do not have the ability to see your final destination. Life is ongoing. If you stay in the same place, where will you ever get to?

I challenge you to go beyond what you see and look for opportunities. Be a boss of your life. Never be fully satisfied. When you fall, rise up. When you cry, begin to smile again, because I can tell you that your life is pretty amazing.

With everything you are, you are fully capable of manifesting an incredible future as a person and athlete. You are divine in your talent and your light shines brighter than you can see. Live your life to the fullest, accept failure, learn from it, and be the best person you can be.

After I thought about many ways to end this book, I arrived at this one. I leave you with this thought: *Your ability to live for today, in the moment, breeding your own future of enlightenment will cause you to remember one thing. That thing is YOU are wonderful, complete, lacking nothing. See the growth you have achieved and carry yourself proudly, because you are a resilient person.*

ABOUT THE AUTHOR

Cate Shepherd is a highly driven and motivated elite soccer player. Her many humbling experiences through soccer have taught her much about the value of patience, hard work, and resilience. She is an extremely competitive young athlete who strives for greatness. Inspired by physical setbacks she endured in 2020, she wrote her first book to share from her heart the wisdom she has learned about what it takes to overcome.

Made in the USA
Monee, IL
07 July 2026

56548206R00056